Invisible War

DISCIPLESHIP SERIES

Angie Meadows

Angie Meadows

A Thousand Tears, LLC
PO Box 1373
Huntington, WV 25715

© 2023 Angie G Meadows

All rights reserved. No portion of this publication may be reproduced, stored in a retrieval system, or transmitted in any form or by any means—electronic, mechanical, photocopy, recording, or any other—without the prior written permission of the author.

I impart to you an indomitable Spirit. Let there be a force that propels your faith to study and grow. May you be strengthened and shielded during times of trouble. I call the fire of the Holy Spirit to burn within in your heart until you are set free by his mighty presence.

Restore unto me the joy of your salvation; and uphold me with your free spirit. Psalm 51:12

Table of Contents

Invisible War 1

1. 2

The Secret Work of the Flesh 2

    Feeble Faith 3

    Healthy Faith 3

    Identify Excuses of your Flesh 11

2. 14

Law of the Spirit of Life vs. Law of Sin and Death 14

    Secrets to Not Quench the Holy Spirit 18

    Study Outline Law of the Spirit of Life 22

3. 25

Conquering our Sin Nature 25

    Adam vs Jesus 26

        Identify Strongholds 26

        War on my Soul 27

4. 34

Understanding Immortality 34

    Flesh 35

    Spirit 35

5. 45

Assurance of Salvation 45

6. 54

Holy Spirit #1 54

7. 66

Holy Spirit #2 66

8. 74

Who am I?	74
God's Responsibility	79
My Responsibility	79
Salvation Pathway	83
Author's Biographies	87
Other Resources by the Author	88
Rock of Recovery Enabler/Addiction	91
Journal Notes	94

1

The Secret Work of the Flesh

The Invisible War

Fellowship with God was a daily and precious blessing in the garden. After the fall, there came a deep-seated aversion for God evidenced by Adam and Eve fleeing and hiding from his presence.

This is characteristic of the "unregenerate nature of the flesh". It is a hidden defect.

This aversion is the hidden work of the flesh against a Holy God. We must seek out areas of our lives that we are **unwilling to surrender** to God.

We must deny and crucify the flesh. *"...He (God) saved us, not because of righteous things we have done, but because of his mercy. He saved us through the washing of rebirth (**regeneration**) and renewal by the Holy Spirit, whom he poured out on us generously through Jesus Christ our Savior, so that, having been **justified** by his grace, we might become heirs having the hope of eternal life." Titus 3:5-6*

*"If any man come after me, he must **deny** himself, and take up his cross, and **follow me**. For whoever will save his life, will lose it, but whoever loses his life for me, will find it." Matthew 16:24-25*

Now learn to **daily walk in the Spirit**. *"...that the righteousness of the law might be fulfilled in us, who walk not after the flesh, but after the Spirit." Romans 8:4*

The greatest sign of this "walking in the flesh" is our feebleness in trusting God.

Feeble Faith	Healthy Faith
Prayerlessness	Prayerful
No desire to read the Word	Watchful
Don't think the Word applies to my life.	Waiting on God
Think God doesn't care or have a plan.	Hunger and thirsting to do God's Will
No vision for the future	Longing for fellowship with Christ
Eyes on the temporal things	Giving up everything for the Pearl of Great Price
Little faith/unbelief	Growing faith
Confusion	Purposeful to develop Fruit of Spirit and good character

Depression	Maturing and unraveling false thinking
Does things to elevate moods	Humbles self and mourns over sin
Fainthearted-Prayers not answered	Steadfast
Feels like giving up	Great Faith

Ask God to identify your hidden aversions to walking with him with your wholeheartedly? These will be the people, things, thoughts, or circumstances (past, present, and future) you have not surrendered to God.

Identifying our Sin Nature by identifying our lust:

...For God cannot be tempted by evil, nor does he tempt anyone; but each one is tempted when, by his own evil desire (lust) he is dragged away and enticed. Then after desire (lust) is conceived, it gives birth to sin; and sin, when it is full grown, gives birth to death. James 1:14-15

There are areas of weaknesses in our lives that need to be identified. After I identify my sinful desires, I can find Scripture to use as a sword to fight my flesh and defeat the lies I believe. Understanding the strength of the flesh is vital to conquering my sin nature by empowering the work of the Holy Spirit in my life. This is done through my cooperation.

If I do not erect boundaries around the weak areas of my life, I will literally be joining forces with Satan and then I will have **three enemies: my flesh, the world, and Satan.** Instead, there needs to be a recognition of my weaknesses and a battle plan to bring every area of life under submission to the Holy Spirit through Scripture mediation and prayer. This will give me great opportunities to stop the vicious cycle of being dragged away.

If I am rationalizing and making excuses for my behavior, thoughts, or words, I am defeated. It has become increasingly apparent to me that I must understand the battle I am fighting. **Sin must be called sin**. Every few weeks, I ask God to show me my hidden defects. It is like an onion. Layer after layer of my heart is exposed.

Ask God to expose the sin in your heart. What do you feel he wants you to <u>confess or forsake</u>?

Seeking for Silver and Searching for Hidden Treasures:
1. Proverbs 15:29 Who does the Lord hear?

Have I aligned myself with righteous thinking in a growing, mature walk?

Or am I feeble and faint-hearted with an unbelieving heart?

2. Ephesians 1:13 After we trust and believe on Christ, what happens?

3. Hebrews 5:14 What do we need to be mature?

How do we get this food?

4. Galatians 5:16 How should we live?

5. Galatians 5:17 What two natures are in conflict in me?

6. Galatians 5:18 How should we be led?

   Can you see a battle between your flesh and spirit?

7. Galatians 5:19-21 List the acts of the sinful nature?

8. Galatians 5:22-23 List the Fruit of the Spirit?

9. Galatians 5:24 Those who belong to Christ do what?

10. Galatians 5:25 How should we live?

11. John 14:16-17 How is the Spirit described?

12. John 14:15 What is the secret to receiving the Spirit?

13. John 14:26 What does the Holy Spirit do for us?

Conclusion

There is a battle raging in our flesh to destroy our souls. Our souls can be described by our mind, will, and emotions. If we are led by our soulish fleshly side, we will do what we feel is right. ***Proverbs 14:12*** *warns us, "There is a way that seems right to a man, but in the end, it leads to death. Paul states in **Romans 6:23** "For the wages of sin is death; but the gift of God is eternal life through Jesus Christ our Lord."*

It never ceases to amaze me, how easily we can fall into temptation. We must be self-controlled and alert and not underestimate the power of the flesh. *Our enemy, the devil, prowls around like a roaring lion looking for someone to devour.* ***I Peter 5:8***. Jesus warns **"Couldn't you men keep watch with me for one hour?" Matthew 26:40** Then he instructs the disciples to *watch and pray*. He tells them what will happen if they don't *"...you will not fall into temptation."* Now Jesus tells them why this type of commitment is so important. *"The spirit is willing, but the flesh is weak." Matthew 26:41*

When I identify my sin and character weaknesses, I know exactly where I am vulnerable and where I will soon stumble if I do not purposefully correct myself.

One of my first steps as a young Christian was to scrutinize my aversion to reading the Scripture and plan for daily devotions.

Soon I recognized my false thinking in the areas of teaching my children Scripture and reading them Bible stories. My thinking was "this isn't my job; it is the church's job". Well, that path of deceptive thinking would have kept us all immature.

"Faith comes by hearing, and hearing by the Word of God." Romans 10:17 Call upon God and ask Him to show you your sins and your weaknesses and give you a sincere desire for the milk of the Word that you may grow and mature in your faith. (1 Peter 2:2) God's says in *Proverbs 8:17, "I love those who love me, and those who seek me, shall find me."*

Now call a trusted friend and discuss the battles you are fighting against your flesh and any aversions or hindrances you may have to studying God's Word.

Application

1. Maturity feeds themselves spiritually.
2. Watching and praying one hour a day will keep us from falling into temptation.
3. When we indulge sin, we are distracted fighting the wrong battle.

Discussion Questions

1. What battles do you need to fight against your own flesh?

2. How can I actively choose to respond with the fruit of the Spirit in every situation in my life?

Identify Excuses of your Flesh
• No one else studies the Bible anymore.
• Sunday is enough. I wouldn't want to be called too religious or narrow.
• I don't understand what I am reading.
• I don't have time.
• I want to but I keep forgetting.
• I can't focus.
• I don't like to read.
• I don't know where I put my Bible.
• My favorite show is on.
• The kids keep interrupting me.
• I fall asleep when I read my Bible.
• I don't know where to start reading.
• It's too overwhelming.

A one time or another, I have made all these excuses. What's your excuse? I remember my grandpa, Earl, sat at the table every night (except church nights) and read his Bible. I remember the peace in his home. I remember how safe I felt when I stayed with my grandparents. At his funeral, people who had worked with him for 40 years at the Steel Plant couldn't remember him ever having an argument with anyone. What a life testimony! Thanks Grandpa!

Father God, grant us the strength to walk out our faith daily. Give us the desire to seek and search for your hidden treasures. Let us correct our false thinking. Lead us to identify lies and excuses and speak a truth in love to one another. Amen.

Now write out your prayer:

Secret Work of the Flesh
Answers

1. God hears the righteous. We talk to him through prayer.
2. We are sealed with the Holy Spirit of Promise.
3. We need to eat solid food.
By constantly exercising and training ourselves to distinguish (discern) between good and evil.
4. If we live by the Spirit, we can say no to the flesh.
5. We have a sinful nature and a Spirit nature.
6. We must stay close enough to the Lord and full of the Holy Spirit so the Spirit to lead us.
7. Sexual immorality, impurity, and debauchery; idolatry and witchcraft; hatred, discord, jealousy, fits of rage, selfish ambition, dissensions, factions, and envy; drunkenness, orgies, and the like.
8. Love, joy, peace, patience, kindness, goodness, faithfulness, gentleness, and self-control.
9. Those who belong to Christ have crucified (put to death) the sinful nature.
10. We should live by the Spirit.
11. The Spirit is described as the comforter/Spirit of Truth. The Spirit lives in us and will abide in us forever.
12. The secret to abiding in the Holy Spirit is to love God and obey his commands.
13. Holy Spirit is the Comforter. His job is to counsel, teach, and remind us of all the things Jesus said.

2

Law of the Spirit of Life vs. Law of Sin and Death

Overcoming Sin and Death

It's an easier journey when our faith comes alive, and the Spirit of the living God lives and breathes in us. This happens as we release the things in our lives that hinder us as our sacrifice for the day. Then we renew our minds by rehearsing the promises of God to ourselves and align our thinking with life and truth.

Walking in the flesh is easily recognizable. It is a life characterized by rehearsing worries, fear, anxiety, bitterness, and produces all kinds of *internal struggles*. This is great emotional suffering.

Our inheritance is peace. If we walk by the Law of the Spirit of Life, we will overcome the Law of Sin and Death which keeps us oppressed. Every moment of everyday we can be rewarded with internal peace and a feeling of great safety. This is the <u>Spirit filled life</u>.

1. Romans 8:1-2 If we are in Christ, what sets us free from the law of sin and death?

*There is no condemnation in Christ Jesus. But it is our responsibility to walk after the Spirit and not the flesh.

2. Romans 8:3 How did the Spirit set me free from sin and death?

3. Romans 8:4 We are not to live according to the

    _____ nature, but according to the

    _____.

4. Romans 8:5 What would it look like if my mind was set on natural things?

5. Romans 8:6 Which mindset is death?

    Which mindset is life?

I know I am controlled by the Spirit of God if I have peace.

What negative emotions are you feeling that are aligned with death?

Pray a prayer and move fear to the altar and exchange it for faith.

6. Romans 8:7 Will sinful (carnal) minds submit to God?

7. Romans 8:8 Can a carnal man please God?

8. Romans 8:9 How can we be controlled by the Spirit of God?

9. Romans 8:10-11 What is our reward?

*The Spirit comes alive through righteousness. Righteousness is just doing the next right thing you know to do.

10. Romans 12:1 How do we worship?

11. Romans 12:2 Do not be _____ any longer to the pattern of this world but be _____ by the renewing your _____.

12. 1 Thessalonians 5:19 What am I not to quench or to put out?

Look at the verses before and after 1 Thessalonians 5:19 (starting at verse 11) for **secrets** to not quenching the Holy Spirit.

Secrets to Not Quench the Holy Spirit
Verse 11
Verse 12
Verse 13
Verse 14.
Verse 15
Verse 16
Verse 17

Verse 18
Verse 20
Verse 21
Verse 22
Verse 23
Verse 24

Conclusion

It is the finished work of the cross that sets us free from the law of sin and death. It is our embracing the mindset of life by transforming our minds through the promises of God's Word to live out our faith that lets us enjoy our daily walk with God.

This is a powerful lesson that will teach us how to think through problems and release them through the power of the Holy Spirit. This power is bigger than us. Learn to trust the Scriptures and find your instructions for an <u>abundant life</u>. *Now unto him that is able to do exceedingly abundantly above all that we ask or think, according to the power that worketh in us, unto him be glory in the church by Christ Jesus throughout all ages, world without end. Amen. Ephesians 3:20-21 KJV*

Application

1. An abundant life is full of peace.
2. Faith moves fear.

Discussion Questions

1. What did it mean when Jesus said, "It is finished?" John 19:30

2. What would it look like to transform my mind.

Father God, give me the freedom to enjoy walking with you daily. Let me embrace the Spirit of Life and cast off the Law of Sin and Death. Let me recognize that fear is the opposite of faith and faith brings me courage and confidence to walk out my abundant destiny in you. Amen.

Write out a prayer:

Study Outline Law of the Spirit of Life

Truths	Instructions
1. Law of Spirit of Life sets you free from the Law of Sin and death. 2. We are set free by the blood of Christ. Christ is our sin offering. 3. Natural mind keeps you in bondage to fear, anxiety, problems, materialism, entertainment, and other distractions. 4. Spirit mind=life and peace 5. Carnal mind= death and fear 6. Carnal mind is hostile to God. 7. Carnal man cannot please God.	1) Live according to the Spirit and not the sin nature. 2) In order to have life and peace the Spirit of God must live in you. 3) Offer your body as a living sacrifice. 4) Renew your mind.
Warning • Do not quench the Spirit of God. • Willful sin will quench God's Spirit. • Do not be conformed to this world. • Do not give wrong for wrong. • Avoid evil.	**Reward** -Life -Peace

Law of the Spirit of Life vs. Law of Sin and Death
Answers

1. Law of Spirit of Life sets us free from the Law of Sin and Death.
2. We are set free by Jesus Christ becoming our sin offering.
3. Flesh nature/Spirit
4. Recognize what you think about most: fear, anxiety, lust, earthly problems, materialistic, entertainment, etc.
5. The carnal mind is controlled by sinful man and is death. Mind controlled by the Spirit is life and peace.
6. No, it is hostile to God.
7. No, it is in the flesh.
8. I can be controlled by the Spirit of God when he lives in me.
9. Life
10. We are to offer our bodies as living sacrifices.
11. Conformed, transformed, mind.
12. <u>Do not quench the Spirit's fire.</u>

Secrets to Not Quench the Holy Spirit (Answers)
Verse 11 Encourage, build up.
Verse 12 Respect those over you
Verse 13 Be at peace among yourselves.
Verse 14 Warn the idle. Encourage the timid. Help the weak. Be patient with everyone.
Verse 15 Don't give evil for evil. Be kind.
Verse 16 Joyful always
Verse 17 Pray continually
Verse 18 Give thanks in all circumstances
Verse 20 Despise not prophesying (preaching)
Verse 21 Test everything, hold to the good.
Verse 22 Avoid every kind of evil.
Verse 23 God will sanctify us. This means he will set us apart. **God will keep us blameless.**
Verse 24 God is faithful.

3

Conquering our Sin Nature

War on the Soul

Why do we sin? According to **Genesis 3**, we understand humans have a fallen nature. Adam and Eve had full reign in the Garden of Eden except they were commanded to not eat from the fruit in the middle of the garden.

Then the serpent showed up and tricked Eve and she disobeyed God and ate from the tree and gave some to her husband, Adam. This caused them to see their nakedness and they were ashamed and hid from God. This separated all of us from our Creator and our spirit died. All of mankind died spiritually in Adam. We would all be born under the curse of sin. We would now need a redeemer, a Savior to reconcile us to God.

1. Romans 5:12 How did sin come into the world?

2. Romans 5:15 How did grace come?

Adam vs Jesus	
Adam = fall of man	**Jesus Christ = sin offering**
Law of sin and death	**Law of the Spirit of Life**
Strongholds	**Confess**
Sinful nature	**Take every thought captive**
Sinful desires	**Ask for wisdom**

Identify Strongholds

3. 2 Corinthians 10:4 What are we fighting against what we need to demolish?

4. 2 Corinthians 10:5 How can we demolish strongholds?

*This is a daily process to continually align our thinking with God's Word. If I am speaking the Word over my life and the promises of God to myself, it is a powerful force to tear down strongholds.

War on my Soul

5. 1 Peter 2:11 What is warring against my soul?

> *Anything drawing me away from Christ and keeping me distracted is waging war on my soul; thoughts, attitudes, behaviors, circumstances...*

6. Romans 7:18 What is my nature?

7. James 1:6-8 What is the weaknesses in these verses?

8. James 1:5 What is the secret to overcoming doubt, double-mindedness, and instability?

9. 2 Corinthians 11:13-14 Who leads us astray?

***<u>We must be grounded in the Word of God so we can rightly divide the Word of God.</u>** 2 Timothy 2:15 Study to show yourself approved unto God, a workman that needs not to be ashamed, rightly dividing the word of truth.*

10. 2 Peter 2:20,22 What is it like if we go back to sin?

11. Romans 13:14 What can we do to keep ourselves from sinning?

Conclusion
We are all prone to distractions and weaknesses and need to understand we are in a battle against our sin nature and learn to empower ourselves through the Holy Spirit to be masters of our internal world. Most of us don't realize we are fighting a battle.

You will always know if you are under the law of Sin and Death because of the fear, anxiety, stress, and other negative emotions will cause internal conflict and suffering.

But when we live under the Law of the Spirit, there will be an alertness to false thinking. We can recognize our peace is missing and find the false belief that is trying to set up a stronghold and tear it down with the truth of God's Word.

It takes time to internally reflect and ask for wisdom and find areas of weaknesses. Only the blood of Jesus can redeem us from the pit of sin. The Holy Spirit is described as the Spirit of Truth and will teach us all things. (John 16:13) All the peace in our lives is a by-product of living in the Spirit.

And let the peace of God rule in your hearts, to the which also you are called in one body; and be thankful. Colossians 3:15

Application

1. A careless Christian will gratify the flesh.
2. A Christian that aligns themselves with foolishness will go into a spiritual slumber and the truth will be taken from him.

Discussion Question

1. What is it like if we return to our sin after we have had a season of enjoying God's peace?

2. What distractions cause you to fall asleep spiritually?
  Ephesians 5:14-15.

Father God, help me to quickly recognize when I have lost my peace. Let me trace my anxiety and fears to its deception that I may break the lies of the enemy. Give me the weapon of prayer and the heart to study to your word that I may wage war against anything that robs my soul of the joy and peace you intended for me. Amen.

Write out your own prayer:

Conquering our Sin Nature
Answers

1. Sin came to the world through one man (Adam).
2. Grace came through the Jesus Christ.
3. Strongholds
4. Identify false thinking or double mindedness that needs to be prayed over and demolished in your life.
5. Sinful desires war against my soul.
6. I have a sinful nature.
7. If I am a doubter and double-minded and this makes me unstable.
8. Ask God for wisdom.
9. False apostles, deceitful workmen, and those pretending to be apostles of Christ lead us astray.
10. It is like a dog returning to its vomit and a washed pig returning to the mud.
11. Do not think about how to gratify the desires of the flesh; instead, clothe yourself in Christ. This is intentionally speaking to yourself differently and with wholesome, healthy words.

4

Understanding Immortality

The Grave of Me, Myself & I

Flesh can't redeem flesh. The mortal flesh must be surrendered to God. This is what I call the "grave of me, myself, and I". I am to have a sanctified holy self that cares for me with strength, courage, and strong personal boundaries. My selfish self must die to everything she ever thought she wanted. As I yield and surrender myself to God, he moves the desires of my heart to match the destiny he has planned for me. This lesson shows us the path to freedom, immorality, and our divine destiny.

1. 1 Corinthians 15:35-37 How are the dead raised?

Flesh	Spirit
1 Corinthians 15:35-57	
Verse 35-36	
Verse 37	
Verse 38	
Verse 39	

2. 1 Corinthians 15:38-41 Compare and contrast different bodies?

Contrast	
Verse 40 Earthly bodies:	
Verse 41 Glory of the sun,	

3. 1 Corinthians 15:42-44 Compare and contrast

Verse 42-44 Sown in corruption.	Raised
Sown in	Raised in
Sown in	Raise in
Natural	Spiritual

4. 1 Corinthians 15:45-49 Can we be earthly and still bear a heavenly image?

Verse 45 1ˢᵗ Adam	Quickening
Verse 46 Natural	Spiritual
Verse 47 From the	From
Verse 49 Bear	Bear

5. 1 Corinthians 15:50-53 Who can inherit the kingdom?

Verse 50 Flesh and _____ cannot inherit the _____	Spirit man can inherit _____
Corruption _____ inherit kingdom	_____ can inherit kingdom
Verse 51 Not all _____	_____ changed
Verse 52 Corruptible	Incorru_____e
Verse 53 Mortal	Immor_____

6. 1 Corinthians 15:54-56 Can I overcome death and the strength of the law?

Verse 54-55 _____ is swallowed up in Victory! O Death, where is your_____? O Grave, where is your _____?
Verse 56 Sting of death is sin. Strength of _____ is the Law

7. 1 Corinthians 15: 57-58 How do we have victory over sin, death, and the grave? Find the instructions. Find the promise.

Gratefulness: Verse 57 But thanks be to _____which give us the victory through our _____.
Instructions: Verse 58 Therefore, my beloved brethren, **be steadfast, unmovable, always abounding in the** _____**of the Lord…**
Promise: Verse 58 Forasmuch as you know that your labor is not in _____**(futile) in the Lord!**

Conclusion

When you are studying Scripture, pull it apart. Don't go too fast. If there is a verse or phrase that piques your interest, there is something in it for you. Write it out and chew on it. Everyday get a verse and carry it with you and repeat it to yourself all day. Let the verse replace any weak voice in your thoughts.

Soak in God's healing Word and let it reshape your mortal flesh into an immortal, non-perishable spiritual person who will be raised by the glory and quickening power through the Spirit of the Law of Life that has conquered the Law of Death and Sin. May each one of you live a victorious life in Christ Jesus, our Lord. Amen.

O death, I declare you swallowed up in Victory.

Application
1. A surrendered heart moves you into your destiny.
2. Studying the Word makes your spirit come alive and your heart burn with the presence of the Holy Spirit.

Discussion Questions
1. Describe your struggles in believing the Bible is true.

2. Describe what it would look like if you were asleep spiritually?

3. What would it look like if you were awake and spiritually hungry?

Father God, give me an insatiable appetite to hunger and thirst for your Word. I declare spiritual growth in knowledge and wisdom as I study your Word. I speak life into my spirit. Let me never go another day without declaring your Word over my loved ones. As I read your written Word, speak into me your living Word. Ignite my heart to burn with your Holy fire. Amen.

Write out declarations of God's Word over your life:

Understanding Immortality
Answers

1. A seed must go into the ground and die to bring forth life. This means we must die to our fleshly/soulish man to bring the Spirit within us alive.

2. There are earthly bodies which are man, beast, fish, birds. Then there are heavenly bodies which is the sun, moon, and the stars, they are different types of bodies.

3. Corrupt: perishable, dishonorable, weak, and natural vs. Incorrupt, non-perishable, glorious, powerful, and spiritual.

4. Yes, we can! Adam: living flesh/soulish, natural and earthly and bearing the image of the earth vs. Jesus: life-giving, spiritual, heavenly, bearing the image of heaven.

5. Those clothed "in" Christ (that is in his immortality) can walk in the Spirit and inherit the Kingdom of God!

6. Yes, I can. I must clothe myself with imperishable and immortality through the Law of the Spirit of Life in Christ Jesus.

7. Victory is through Jesus.

Instructions: Stand firm and let nothing move you.

Promise: Know that your labor in the Lord isn't in vain

Outline

Flesh	Spirit
1 Corinthians 15:35-57	
Verse 35-36 Can't be raised unless it dies	Raised
Verse 37 grain	Must bury flesh
Verse 38 Every kind of seed has its own body	
Verse 39 Man, beast, fish, birds	
Contrast	
Verse 40 Earthly bodies: people, animals, birds, and fish	Celestial (heavenly) bodies
Verse 41 Glory of the sun, moon, stars, they are all different.	
Resurrection of the Dead	
Verse 42-44 Sown corruption (perishable)	Raised in incorruption (non-perishable)
Sown in Dishonor	Raised in glory
Sown in Weakness	Raise in power
Natural Body	Spiritual Body
Verse 45 1st Adam (Living Soul)	Quickening (life-giving) spirit
Verse 46 Natural (Adam, earth/earthly man)	Spiritual (Lord from Heaven/Jesus)

Verse 47 From the dust of the earth	From heaven
Verse 49 Bear image earthly	Bear image heavenly
Verse 50 Flesh and blood cannot inherit the kingdom	Spirit man can inherit kingdom
Corruption cannot inherit kingdom	Incorruption can inherit kingdom
Verse 51 Sleep	Not all sleep, but be changed
Verse 52 Corruptible	Incorruptible
Verse 53 Mortal	Immortality. Dead will be raised.
Verse 54-55 **Death has been swallowed up in victory. O Death, where is your sting? O death where is your victory?**	
Verse 56 Sting of death is sin. Strength of sin is the Law.	
Gratefulness: Verse 57 But thanks be to God, which give us the victory through our Lord Jesus Christ.	
Instructions: Verse 58 Therefore, my beloved brethren, **be steadfast, unmovable, always abounding in the work of the Lord…**	
Promise: Verse 58 Forasmuch as you know that your labor is not in vain (futile) in the Lord!	

5

Assurance of Salvation

If the Lord says it, I believe it.

Freedom to be a doer of the Word and not just a hearer is a progressive journey to subdue the flesh until we receive grace. *Now, sin shall not have dominion over you because we are not under the law but under grace. Romans 6:14*

God's Word is true and if the Lord says it, I can believe it. God won't forget my faithfulness to him. Nor will he forget his promises to me.

If I stop believing because of a trauma or some bad circumstance, this will stunt my progress. I must practice receiving his grace and ask for the Lord to be my redeemer. *And he said unto me, my grace is sufficient for you: for my strength is made perfect in weakness. Most gladly therefore will I rather glory in my infirmities, that the power of Christ may rest upon me. 2 Corinthians 12:9* Today, it is time to know the love of my redeemer. *(God) who redeems my life from destruction (is he) who crowns me with lovingkindness and tender mercies. Psalm 103:4*

Get a vision for your infinite worth. Know your value in the father's eyes. Let him restore, redeem, comfort, heal and make you whole again. Let the father assure you of your salvation in him.

1. James 1:25 How will we know when the Word of God is truly coming alive in our hearts?

2. James 1:26 How do we know we are out of step with God?

Matthew 15:18 But those things which proceed out of the mouth come forth from the heart, and they defile the person.

3. Matthew 12:34 How do I know what is in my heart that I need to deal with?

4. Romans 8:11 Can we have assurance that we will be resurrected like Christ?

5. Hebrews 6:10 Is God forgetful of what you have done for Him?

6. Hebrews 6:12 What will we, who follow Christ, inherit?

7. Romans 2:7a What does God expect us to do?

8. Romans 2:7b What is the promise?

9. Ephesians 2:10 Why were we created?

10. John 10:29 Can we have assurance of salvation?

11. 1 John 3:20 What if I don't feel saved?

> *Father, assure me of my salvation. Let me doubt no more.*

12. 1 John 4:4 Can I overcome the world?

13. Ephesians 1:13 Who does God give us when we believe?

Conclusion

The promise is eternal life through Christ Jesus. The Word of the Lord assures us that we were created for good works. When I trust in the promises of God, knowing that nothing and no one can pluck me out of the hand of God I am safe. I am free to grow in the understanding that greater is he that is in me than he that is in the world. He is greater than my negative internal critic. He is greater than my guilt, shame, and self-condemnation. He is greater than any circumstance in my life. I can trust my Lord to never leave me or forsake me.

The Lord Jesus tells us in John 16:33 that he has overcome the world and he gave us the Holy Spirit to seal us with the promise. How will any of us navigate life's difficulties without the hope of a better day? Rest in the assurance that salvation is a gift from God for me, you, and our entire households. Know that once he has begun a good work in you, he will finish it. Philippians 1:6

Application

1. God is able to finish what he started in me. No matter how much wavering I have done in the past.
2. God is greater than any of my temporal problems.

Discussion Questions

1. Do I rehearse the promises of God more or do I stand firm and declare his promises over my life?

2. Ask the Lord to show you any lie you believe about yourself.

Lord, Jesus, let not sin have dominion over me. Loose me from ungodly strongholds. When life's struggles start to get the best of me, give me more grace. Grace to move forward. Grace to continue believing. Amen.

Write out your own prayer:

Assurance of Salvation
Answers

1. We won't forget. We will be free to be doers and not just hearers.
2. If our religion is worthless it will show up in our speech. The mouth speaks what is in our hearts.
3. Listen to your own words. You will hear the bitterness you need to deal with. You will doubt the assurance of salvation if you hold onto junk in your life. Let it go and make room to experience the fullness of God's salvation through his presence. It won't change the status of your salvation; but it will change you.
4. Yes, because God's Word says we will.
5. No, God will not forget.
6. We will inherit the promises.
7. He expects us to consistently do good and seek glory, honor, and immortality. *He wants us to seek things of eternal value and not to spin our tails circling in the wilderness of unbelief. Just believe that everything was meant for your good and God's glory. Romans 8:28
8. He will give eternal life.
9. We were created for good works.
10. Yes, no man can take us out of the Father's hand.
11. God is greater than our heart. Stand on God's Word, not on your emotions.
12. Yes, because greater is He that is in you, than he that is in the world.
13. The Lord gives us the Holy Spirit.

6

Holy Spirit #1

Peace, I leave with you.

Don't miss the second baptism, which is the baptism of the Holy Spirit. The first is water baptism. God, the father's, one message when John the Baptist baptized Jesus was "You are my Son, whom I love, with you I am well pleased." Mark 1:11 Later Jesus says, it is good that I go away so the Comforter, the Holy Spirit, will come. John 16:7

After we are born again, there is more. Believers consistently yearn to be with other believers in fellowship and help each other grow in the fruit of the Spirit.

1. Mark 1:8 What is John saying Jesus will baptize us with?

2. Mark 1:10-11 Who does the dove represent?

3. Matthew 18:18-20 How will Jesus be amid us?

4. John 3:5 What two ways do we need to be born to enter the kingdom?

5. Galatians 5:22-25 What will we look like if we are born of the Spirit?

6. John 3:19-21 Will those who love darkness come to church with you?

7. John 4:24 How are we to worship God?

8. Outline John 14
   A. Vs. 15 What will we do if we love Jesus?

   B. Vs. 16 Who will He give us?

   C. Vs. 17 What is the Holy Spirit referred to?

   D. Vs. 18 What is the promise?

E. Vs. 19 What else will this Holy Spirit give us?

F. Vs. 20 Can we abide (be one) with Christ?

G. Vs. 21 How can we have God manifested to us?

H. Vs. 22-23 Jesus will abide with which people?

I. Vs. 26 What will the Holy Spirit do?

J. Vs. 27 What is the promise? What is the admonishment?

Godly (Holy Spirit) peace is the confident assurance in any circumstance. (John 14:27)

---

9. John 16:7 Why was it important that Jesus went away?

10. John 16:8 What will the Holy Spirit do?

11. John 16:13 Holy Spirit is referred to as what?

John 14 Outline
1. Verse 15 Those who love the Lord will keep his_____.
2. Verse 16 The _____ is referred to as a Comforter (Advocate).
3. Verse 17 The Holy Spirit is the Spirit of_____
4. Verse 18 Promise: The _____ is the fulfillment of the promise of his presence. He won't leave us orphans!
5. Verse 19 The Holy Spirit is _____.
6. Verse 20 Through the Holy Spirit we can be with Christ.

7. Verse 21 The _____ will empower us to keep his commands and then Jesus will show himself to us.
8. Verse 22-23 Jesus will abide with them through the _____ who obey Him.
9. Verse 26 _____ will be our comforter (advocate), teach, bring to remembrance Christ's teachings.
10. Verse 27 **Promise:** _____
11. Verse 27 **Instruction:** The gentle chiding is for me to _____ let my heart be troubled or to be afraid.
12. Verse 27: Application: God sized (Holy Spirit) _____ is the confident assurance in any circumstance.

Conclusion

The precious Holy Spirit is our guide, teacher, comforter and the one who brings us life. During conflict and stress, we can find peace, and experience the presence of the Holy Spirit.

The Holy Spirit brings us into union as one with the Father, Son, and Holy Spirit. He will never leave us or forsake us. (Hebrews 13:5) He will finish the good work he started within us. (Philippians 1:6) Learning to walk in love through the Holy Spirit will cast out fear and we can have a life without torment. (1 John 4:18)

Lord, give me your peace, help my heart not to be troubled or afraid. If I am troubled, help me to recognize your Spirit and have the

Holy Spirit remind me of your Words. Strengthen me to remain in your love. In Jesus name, Amen

Application
1. When I walk with the Holy Spirit I will not feel like an orphan.
2. I will have peace when I am walking with the Holy Spirit.

Discussion Questions
1. On a scale of 1-10 describe your daily level of anxiety last week.

2. What would it look like if I didn't let my heart be troubled about anything?

Holy Spirit be my comforter, my teacher, and my guide. Strengthen me according to your Word. Engraft your Word in me that I may cast out fear and torment and live an abundant life and enjoy my inheritance of peace. Heal my anxious grieving heart and teach me to allow you to comfort me every day.

Write out your own prayer. Ask the Holy Spirit to come into your life in a baptismal measure.

Holy Spirit #1
Answers

1. Jesus will baptize us with the Holy Spirit.
2. The dove is a symbol of the Holy Spirit.
3. When we gather and pray the presence of the Lord is with us.
4. Born of water (possibly infers physical birth) and born of the spirit this infers a spiritual awakening.
5. We will have the fruit of the Spirit and be progressively growing in love, joy, peace, long-suffering (patience), gentleness, goodness, faith, meekness, temperance (self-control).
6. No. They don't want truth (light) to expose their sin. Who is the light? Jesus (truth).
7. In Spirit and in truth, this is opposed to worshipping God with our carnal mind and nature.
8.   A. Keep His commandments.
      B. The Holy Spirit is referred to as a Comforter (Advocate).
      C. The Holy Spirit is referred to the Spirit of truth.
      D. Jesus says he will come to us through the Holy Spirit.
      E. The Holy Spirit is life.
      F. Yes, we can be one with Christ.
      G. God will manifest himself to us if we keep His commandments.
      H. Jesus will abide with them who choose to obey Him.
      I. Holy Spirit will be our comforter (advocate), teach, bring to remembrance Christ's teachings.
      J. Peace. The gentle chiding is for me to not let my heart be troubled or to be afraid.
9. Jesus had to go away so the comforter, the Holy Spirit, could come.
10. The Holy Spirit convict us of sin.

11. The Holy Spirit is referred to the Spirit of truth and will guide you into all truth.

John 14 Outline
1. Verse 15 Those who love the Lord will keep his commands.
2. Verse 16 The Holy Spirit is referred to as a Comforter (Advocate).
3. Verse 17 The Holy Spirit is the Spirit of Truth.
4. Verse 18 Promise: The Holy Spirit is the fulfillment of the promise of his presence. He won't leave us orphans!
5. Verse 19 The Holy Spirit is life.
6. Verse 20 Through the Holy Spirit we can be one with Christ.
7. Verse 21 The Holy Spirit will empower us to keep his commands and then Jesus will show himself to us.
8. Verse 22-23 Jesus will abide with them through the Holy Spirit who obey Him.
9. Verse 26 Holy Spirit will be our comforter (advocate), teacher, and bring to remembrance Christ's teachings.
10. Verse 27 Promise: **Peace**
11. Verse 27 Instruction: The gentle chiding is for me to <u>not</u> let my heart be troubled or to be afraid.
12. Verse 27: Application: Godly (Holy Spirit) <u>peace</u> is the confident assurance in any circumstance.

7

Holy Spirit #2

The Spirit of Adoption cries Abba, Father.

There are three commands for the new disciple of Jesus Christ. The first command is to come. Matthew 11:28 The second is to follow. Matthew 9:9 The Lord directs our hearts with peace, we can hear his voice and easily follow his direction. The third instruction is to abide or to dwell with him as one. We can't do this without the Holy Spirit. John 15:4

These studies are to give us an awareness of this beautiful gift. When we truly learn to abide in Christ, our hearts will be aligned with his and we can ask whatever we want, and he will give it to us. This sounds impossible. But when I am walking as <u>one</u> with the Lord, my heart knows where he is leading me and is full of a vision for my future.

1. Romans 8:15 What are the two Spirits in this verse?

How can we know what Spirit we are following?

The Spirit of Adoption we will cry out to Abba, Father in our need.

---

2. Romans 8:17-18 Can we expect suffering in this life?

If we suffer with him, we will also be what?

What shall be revealed in us after suffering?

3. 2 Corinthians 1:20-22
   Vs. 20 What is "yes" (for sure) in this verse?

Vs. 21 Who establishes us (makes us to stand firm)?

Vs. 22 How can we really know for sure?

4. 1 John 4:6 What are the two spirits in this verse?

5. 1 Corinthians 2:10 Spirit brings what with Him?

Vs. 11 What can we expect to know if we have the Spirit of God?

Vs. 12 What other spirit is there?

If we have God's Spirit, will we know the things of God?

Vs. 13 What are the two kinds of wisdom?

Vs. 14 Can the carnal man receive wisdom?

What will God's wisdom be to the worldly person?

Vs. 15 What can a Holy Spirit filled man discern?

Vs. 16 Can we have the mind of Christ?

How?

Conclusion

The Spirit of Adoption brings us into the family of God with a father with tender loving kindness. This father is full of kindness and always ready to forgive. The Lord calls for us to come up under the shadow of his wings for protection. He tells us that he is our provider and our redeemer. That we are bought by him. Purchased with the blood of Jesus Christ and that salvation is a gift for anyone who will receive it.

Spirit of Adoption	Spirit of Bondage
1. Confident	Fearful
2. Crying Abba Father	Orphan spirit
3. Suffering=glory	Suffering=anxiety
4. Down payment of the Holy Spirit	Easily Deceived
5. Spirit of Truth	Spirit of Error
6. Revelation=Understanding things of God	Man's Wisdom
7. Holy Spirit's Wisdom	Foolishness
8. Mind of Christ	Carnal Mind

Application

1. Adoption into the family of God gives us a confident assurance that we are loved.
2. A carnal person will embrace a spirit of error and be easily deceived.

Discussion Questions

1. What would I need to do to develop the mind of Christ?

2. Can I discern when others aren't ready to receive truth?

Holy Spirit, develop in me the gift of understanding. That I may be wiser than my teachers. Give me a gentle spirit that is patient and easy to entreat and apt to loving teach others as I correct myself. Give me your Word as a lamp unto my feet and a light unto my path. Amen

Write out your own prayer and ask for understanding in one area of your life that feels needy or out of balance.

Holy Spirit #2
Answers

1. Spirit of slavery (bondage) and the Spirit of Adoption.
If we follow the Spirit of Bondage, we will be fearful. If we follow the Spirit of Adoption, we will confidence in God.

2. Yes.
We will be glorified with him.
Glory.

3. **Verse 20** The promises of God are sure.
   Verse 21 God.
   Verse 22 Because He will give us a down payment in our hearts.
   The down payment is the Holy Spirit.

4. The Spirit of truth and the Spirit of falsehood (error).

5. **Verse 10** Revelation.
Verse 11 We will understand the things of God.
Verse 12 Spirit of this world.
Yes
Verse 13 Man's wisdom can teach us, or the Holy Spirit's wisdom can teach us.
Verse 14 Yes, but it is man's wisdom.
Foolishness.
Verse 15 A Holy Spirit filled person can discern Truth vs. Error.
Verse 16 Yes, we can have the mind of Christ.
We can have the mind of Christ through the (Holy) Spirit

8

Who am I?

May Rivers of Living Water Flow from your Belly

Until I know who I am in Christ, I will be pushed around in the rapids of the river of life. It's likely that I will feel like I don't even have a paddle to steer and am constantly pushed against the rocks and my entire focus is just to stay upright. The truth is that I can know my God through the Holy Spirit and have rivers of living waters flowing out of my belly. John 7:38

When I know who I am in Christ, I steer my thoughts with the Promises of God's Word. I speak to myself with gentleness and kindness. I trust that God's ways are higher, and his thoughts are higher than mine, how could I possibly know them. Isaiah 55:9 My journey is to grow my faith and to pursue him in every area of my life.

This is a faith walk. A walk that will lead me to a relationship with Christ to be **mighty** in the Spirit Zechariah 4:6 or it will lead me to a life of wandering in the wilderness of unbelief. The pressures of life are to bring me to an awareness of my need for Christ and allow the

Lord to be my Savior, my deliverer, my rock, and the horn of my salvation. Psalms 18:2

1. John 1:12 Who am I?

    What is my responsibility?

Truth: This is not a natural birth by a man's will but born of God.

2. John 15:15 Who am I to Christ?

When I begin to hang out with Christ and fellowship with Him, what is the promise?

3. Romans 5:1 How can we be reconciled (justified) with God?

4. 1 Corinthians 6:17 Who does God want me to unite (join) with and why?

Because I will be one spirit with Him. In 1 Corinthians 6:12 it indicates that this adjoining our self with Christ will empower us not to be mastered, overpowered, or controlled by anything.

5. Ephesians 1:1 How does Paul address believers?

6. Ephesians 1:5 How can we become saints?

7. Ephesians 2:17-18 How do we have access to the father? Read Ephesians 2:13

8. Colossians 1:14 Do I have to carry my guilt anymore?

   Read Colossians 1:12-13

9. Colossians 2:10 What have I been given in Christ?

Conclusion

This is a faith walk. It isn't a walk by sight, but a walk by faith. 2 Corinthians 5:7

Now, learn to recognize the flesh and how it distracts you off into self-absorption and a place of feeling like an orphan without a father where you feel like hiding.

There are no orphans in the kingdom of God. There is a reliance and total dependency upon a faithful father. We just come to him with childlike faith. Luke 18:17

God's Responsibility God says I am:	My Responsibility I Must:
1. His Child.	1. Open my heart to receive.
2. His friend.	2. Know and grow in the Father's Business.
3. One with him in the Spirit	3. Pursue Peace.
4. A Holy people.	4. Remain faithful in Jesus Christ.
5. Predestined for Adoption	5. Learn to exercise my power and Authority through Christ.
6. In the fullness in Christ.	
7. Full of his assurance and peace.	
8. Redeemed.	
9. Forgiven.	

Application
1. Knowing who I am in Christ, gives me confidence.
2. If I am wandering in the wilderness, I need to address my unbelief.

Discussion Questions

1. What area of my life do I need to activate my faith by surrendering the outcomes to the Lord?

2. How easily can I steer my thoughts?

3. Do I know how to preach the Word of God to myself until I get a breakthrough?

Lord, I don't know what you are doing, but I trust you. Help me to trust you more and more. Help me move the noisy stuff of confusion and put it in its proper place under our feet. Make me a new creation in Christ Jesus.

Turn a Scripture into a prayer:

Who Am I?
Answers

1. I am God's child.
I am to receive him.
2. I am His friend.
The promise is that he will make known to me the things from the father.
3. We are justified through faith through the Lord Jesus Christ. Pray for this gift of faith.
4. Lord (Jesus)
Because I will be one spirit with Him. In 1 Corinthians 6:12 it indicates that this adjoining our self with Christ will empower us not to be mastered, overpowered, or controlled by anything.
5. Paul addresses believers as "Saints" who are faithful in Christ Jesus.
6. It is God's pleasure that adopts us into His family through Jesus Christ, His Son.
7. We have access through Jesus Christ.
8. No, in Christ Jesus we have redemption and forgiveness of sins. Read Colossians 1:12-13
9. I have been given the fullness (completeness) in Christ. Jesus Christ is head over every power and authority.

Salvation Pathway

If you have not received Christ as your Savior and you would like to do so or would like to rededicate your heart to Him, here is the Salvation Pathway Scriptures to study.

1. John 3:16 What is our responsibility?

2. Romans 3:23 Why do we need a Savior?

3. Romans 6:23 If we turn from our sin, what is the promise?

4. Romans 10:9 What is my responsibility?

5. Romans 10:13 How can I be saved?

6. Romans 10:17 How can I increase my faith?

7. Revelation 3:20 Who wants to come into our lives and fellowship with us?

8. Ephesians 2:8 How are we saved?

It is in surrender that we find the peace of Christ.

Salvation Pathway
Answers

1. Believe
2. We have all sinned.
3. The gift of God is eternal life through Jesus Christ our Lord.
4. Confess with my mouth the Lord Jesus
Believe in my heart that God raised him from the dead.
5. Call (pray)
6. Faith comes by hearing God's Word.
7. Jesus
8. For by grace are you saved through faith; it is a gift of God.

Lord, open my heart for salvation. Help me to believe, truly believe that I can trust you and have confidence in you and that I don't need to carry the burdens of this world alone. Give me the gift of eternal life through your Son, and his finished work on the cross. Teach me to live and walk by faith daily. Teach me to pray. Teach me to trust you more and more. Amen.

Write out a prayer and ask for forgiveness and redemption through the blood of Christ in every area of your life that still needs surrendered.

Author's Biographies

Angie Meadows is an ordained minister. She is currently a mother, grandmother, speaker, and writer. Her favourite pastime is quilting and discipling others. She is currently recording podcasts, and radio shows called Rock of Recovery to teach Developmental Emotional Maturity Skills and along with these Bible studies to disciple others to grow in Christ.

Other Resources by the Author

Bible Studies

1. Seven Pillars of Wisdom ISBN: 9781732810297

Seven Pillars of Wisdom. Wisdom has built her house; she has hewn out its seven pillars. This is a verse-by-verse study from Proverbs. The fear of the Lord is wisdom: understanding, discernment, truth, righteousness, knowledge, instruction, and prudence. These words will be thoroughly studied. This is an individual, small group Sunday School, Christian school Bible full semester Bible Study with multiple challenges at the end to develop your own studies and to mine for great treasures from the Word of God. Ages 13 and above.

2. The Daniel Study ISBN:9798987429037

This book has the first 6 chapters of Daniel come alive for studies while studying the character skill that Daniel and his three friends needed to overcome their troubles. Each lesson has thinking principle, character skill, ten or more questions for the student to answer, self-evaluation section for applying what we are learning and a parent/teacher suggestion section. Ages 7 and above. A great beginner Bible study for any new Christian.

Enabler Recovery Books

1. A Thousand Tears: An Enabler's Journey ISBN 9781732810204

This is the same book as Enabler's Journey: A Christian Perspective, but it is written with principles and not Scriptures.

The book identifies the Enabler's Cycle and our conflict with individuals with addiction. Identifying manipulative, devouring, or toxic relationships in our life and learning to confront and detach. It also includes multiple self-assessment tools: Enabler's paradigm, entanglement gauge, anxiety quotient, trust scales, and much more.

2. An Enabler's Journey: A Christian Perspective ISBN: 9781732810211

This book is 300+ pages and 24 chapters. It is almost the same book as *A Thousand Tear: An Enabler's Journey* except it has a 100+ Scriptures to validate the principles for dealing with difficult people in relationships. This book will convince the elderly Christian family members to stop enabling.

3. Enabler's Journey Recovery Plan Enabler's Journey Recovery Series: Book 1 ISBN: 9781732810228

This is a 100+ page Book One of a recovery workbook series. It guides individuals and clients to understand enabling behaviours and evaluate their current participation in perpetuating a person with substance use disorder's illness. The enabler will learn to recognize the cycle of enabling, entanglement, excuses, and beliefs that handicap an enabler from recovery.

4. Enabler's Journey Detachment Enabler's Journey Recovery Series Book 2 ISBN: 9781732810235

This book empowers us to learn survival skills with 12 DETACHMENT PRINCIPLES. This book is a useful tool in dealing with substance use disorder, or other individuals with abusive or irresponsible behaviours. It includes many self-assessment tools:

Rock of Recovery Enabler/Addiction
Developmental Emotional Maturity Skills

1. Rock of Recovery Anxiety Trap ISBN:9781732810242

Painful emotions drive toxic relationships and addictive behaviors. Conquering anxiety, finding a safe self internally, learning to break a helpless/victim trap with disciplined thinking, uncovering hidden emotions under the cloak of anxiety, overcoming doublemindedness, and internally finding rest and peace are just a few developmental emotional skills.

2. Rock of Recovery Overcoming Torment ISBN 9781732810266

Unresolved anxiety can become passive tormented thinking, which ends with trauma. Now, let us unravel these dysfunctional thinking patterns and gain emotional maturity. This book teaches us to recognize trauma, its triggers, inner core emotional responses and its severe behavioral responses along with accompanying mental prisons and mind control holding us captive.

3. Rock or Recovery Overcoming Trauma ISBN:9781732810273

In this book we learn how to identify our trauma wounds and inner core responses and recognize, release, and retrain our emotions. There will be a trauma trap evaluation, a mood tracer, understanding mental prisons, mind control, a higher ground emotional trainer, thought regulator, understanding healthy love, finding joy, peace, patience, gentleness, spiritual sickness, feeble vs. healthy faith, and finding freedom in self-control.

4. Rock of Recovery Spirit and Soul Disconnect ISBN: 9781732810280

Rock of Recovery Spirit and Soul Disconnect. Anything that causes you suffering, or anxiety is a disconnect. We disconnect from our true self and connect to anxiety and other emotional suffering. This causes us to abandon our own self.

5. Rock of Recovery Reconciliation ISBN: 9798987429006

Rock of Recovery Reconciliation This book is specifically written for families to reconcile with loved ones returning from addiction recovery programs or prison.

6. Rock of Recovery Detachment ISBN: 979898429013

This book teaches the 12 Detachment Principles throughout Scripture to develop a healthy identity and healthy boundaries.

7. Rock of Recovery Relationship Addiction ISBN: 979-8-9874290-4-4

Four relationship addiction levels: codependency, relational dependency, trauma bonding, and relationship bondage with the relationship behavioral addiction cycles. We will learn why we repeat toxic relationship cycles and how to break free.

Rule and Reign your Internal World

Developmental Emotional Maturity Skills for anyone age 14 and above.

**1. Rule and Reign your Internal World: Defeating Anxiety
ISBN:9781732810259**

This is the same information as the Rock of Recovery Series for Enablers and those with substance use disorder. It is reorganized for anyone needing Developmental Emotional Maturity Skills.

**2. Rule and Reign Your Internal World Overcoming Torment
ISBN: 979-8-9874290-2-0**

This is the same information as the Rock of Recovery Overcoming Torment for Enablers and those with substance use disorder. It is reorganized for anyone needing Developmental Emotional Maturity Skills. This series is an individual devotional, home-school, or Christian School curriculum, Family Devotions, or Small Group anxiety study. Ages 14 and above.

Kindle eBooks available for all titles.

Angie Meadows

Journal Notes

Invisible War

Angie Meadows

Invisible War

www.ingramcontent.com/pod-product-compliance
Lightning Source LLC
Chambersburg PA
CBHW060340050426
42449CB00011B/2801